KU-049-438

To:

From:

Date:

Message:

Treasures

OF INSPIRATION

HELEN STEINER RICE

christian
art gifts

Treasures of inspiration

Compiled by Virginia J. Ruehlmann

© 2002 Christian Art Gifts, PO Box 1599, Vereeniging, 1930, South Africa

ISBN 1-86920-049-7

Printed in Singapore

02 03 04 05 06 07 08 09 10 11 – 10 9 8 7 6 5 4 3 2 1

One place to go

The Lord is the strength of his people,
he is the saving refuge of his anointed.
Psalm 28:8 RSV

When we feel we have nothing left to give
and we're sure that the song has ended.
When our day seems
over and shadows fall
and the darkness of night has descended,
Where can we go to find the strength
to valiantly keep on trying?
Where can we find the hand that will dry
the tears that the heart is crying?
There's but one place
to go and that is to God.

A healing touch

My hand will sustain him; surely
my arm will strengthen him.
Psalm 89:21 NIV

Sorrow, which we dread so much
can bring a very healing touch
For when we fail to heed God's voice
we leave the Lord no other choice
Except to use a firm, stern hand
to make us know He's in command.

Our acceptance

God is our refuge and strength,
a very present help in trouble.
Psalm 46:1 RSV

Blessed are the people
who learn to accept
The trouble we try to escape and reject,
For in our acceptance
we're given great grace
And courage and faith
and the strength to face
The daily troubles that come to us all,
So we may learn to
stand straight and tall.
For the grandeur of life
is born of defeat,
For in overcoming
we make life complete.

7

Widen my vision

Restore to me the joy of
your salvation and grant me
a willing spirit, to sustain me.
Psalm 51:12 NIV

God, widen my vision so I may see
The affliction You have sent to me
Not as a cross too heavy to wear
That weighs me down in gloomy despair,
Not as something to hate and despise
But a gift to love sent in disguise.

Willing to yield

*I am not saying this because I am
in need, for I have learned to be content
whatever the circumstances.*
Philippians 4:11 NIV

Trouble is something
no one can escape –
Everyone has it in some form or shape.
But the wise person
accepts whatever God sends,
Willing to yield
like a storm-tossed tree bends,
Knowing that God
never made a mistake,
So whatever He sends
be willing to take.

God's reassurance

Even to your old age and gray hairs I am
he, I am he who will sustain you. I have
made you and I will carry you; I will
sustain you and I will rescue you.
Isaiah 46:4 NIV

Whatever betide you,
God is always beside you,
So "let not your heart be troubled"
nor your mind be filled with fear,
For you have God's reassurance
that He's always very near.

Standing by

*Even though I walk through the valley
of the shadow of death, I will fear no
evil, for you are with me; your rod
and your staff, they comfort me.*
Psalm 23:4 NIV

There are times when life overwhelms us
and our trials seem too many to bear –
It is then we should stop to remember
God is standing by ready to share
The uncertain hours that confront us
and fill us with fear and despair.

You are near

Ask and it will be given to you;
seek and you will find; knock and
the door will be opened to you.
Matthew 7:7 NIV

My blessings are so many,
my troubles are so few –
How can I be discouraged
when I know that I have You?
And I have the sweet assurance
that there's nothing I need fear
If I but keep remembering
I am Yours and You are near.

Undaunted

And we desire each one of you to show
the same earnestness in realizing the
full assurance of hope until the end.
Hebrews 6:11 RSV

If I remain undaunted though
the billows sweep and roll,
Knowing I have Your assurance,
there's a haven for my soul ...
For anything and everything
can somehow be endured
If Your presence is beside me
and lovingly assured.

Sincere prayer

*Such is the confidence that we
have through Christ toward God.*
2 Corinthians 3:4 RSV

I'm so unsure of just how to pray –
To tell You the truth, God,
I don't know what to say.
I just know
I'm lonely and vaguely disturbed,
Bewildered and restless,
confused and perturbed,
And they tell me
that prayer helps to quiet the mind
And to unburden the heart,
for in stillness we find
someone does care
And Someone does answer
each small, sincere prayer.

The key to the future

*Let us draw near with a true heart in full
assurance of faith, with our hearts
sprinkled clean from an evil conscience
and our bodies washed with pure water.*
Hebrews 10:22 RSV

God in His goodness has promised
that the cross that He gives us to wear
Will never exceed our endurance
or be more than our strength can bear.
And secure in that blessed assurance,
we can smile as we face tomorrow,
For God holds the key to the future,
and no sorrow or care we need borrow.

Deeply burdened

*Is not your fear of God
your confidence, and the integrity
of your ways your hope?*
Job 4:6 RSV

I tell Him I am heartsick
and lost and lonely, too,
That my mind is deeply burdened
and I don't know what to do.
But I know He stilled the tempest
and calmed the angry sea,
And I humbly ask if, in His love,
He'll do the same for me.

Through God's eyes

Be exalted, O Lord, in thy strength!
We will sing and praise thy power.
Psalm 21:13 RSV

Seen through God's eyes,
earthly troubles diminish
And we're given new faith
to face and to finish
Life's daily tasks as they come along
If we pray for strength to keep us strong
So go to our Father
when troubles assail you,
For His grace is sufficient
and He'll never fail you.

Thoughts of peace

*In the fear of the Lord one
has strong confidence, and his
children will have a refuge.*
Proverbs 14:26 RSV

Anything and everything
can some way be endured
Because God's presence is
beside me and lovingly assured.
So I will just keep quiet and
think only thoughts of peace,
For if I abide in stillness,
my restless murmurings cease.

His purpose

*It is better to take refuge in the
Lord than to put confidence in man.*
Psalm 118:8 RSV

While it's very difficult for
mankind to understand
God's intensions and His purpose
and the workings of His hand.
If we observe the miracles
that happen every day,
We cannot help but be convinced
that in His wondrous way
God makes what
seemed unbearable
and painful and distressing
Easily acceptable
when we view it as a blessing.

Our attitudes

*Your attitude should be
the same as that of Christ Jesus.*
Philippians 2:5 NIV

The nature of our attitudes
toward circumstantial things
Determines our acceptance
of the problems that life brings,
And since fear and dread
and worry cannot help in any way,
It's much healthier and happier
to be cheerful every day.
And if you'll only try it,
you will find, without a doubt,
A cheerful attitude's something
no one should be without.

Adversity

My flesh and my heart may fail,
but God is the strength of my
heart and my portion for ever.
Psalm 73:26 RSV

The way we use adversity
is strictly our own choice.
For in God's hands adversity
can make the heart rejoice.
For everything God sends to us,
no matter in what form,
Is sent with plan and purpose,
for by the fierceness of a storm
The atmosphere
is changed and cleared
and the earth is washed and clean,
And the high winds of adversity
can make restless souls serene.

Thy way

Forgive my hidden faults.
Psalm 19:12 NIV

Forgive the many errors
that I made yesterday
And let me try again, dear God,
to walk closer to Thy way.

Forgiven

If you forgive anyone his sins,
they are forgiven; if you do not
forgive them, they are not forgiven.
John 20:23 NIV

It's true that
the great, generous Savior
forgives our transgressions
each day
And patiently waits
for lost sheep
who constantly
seem to stray

Grant us strength

I cry out to God Most High, to God,
who fulfills his purpose for me.
Psalm 57:2 NIV

Bless us, heavenly Father –
forgive our erring ways.
Grant us strength to serve Thee,
put purpose in our days.
Give us understanding,
enough to make us kind,
So we may judge all people
with our hearts and not our minds.

Your faithful friend

*Let the wicked forsake his way
and the evil man his thoughts.
Let him turn to the Lord, and he
will have mercy on him, and to
our God, for he will freely pardon.*
Isaiah 55:7 NIV

God forgives until the end –
He is your faithful, loyal Friend
He's ever-present and always there
To take you in His tender care.
And bind the wounds
and mend the breaks
When all the world
around forsakes.

Making amends

*Fools mock at making
amends for sin, but goodwill is
found among the upright.*
Proverbs 14:9 NIV

As each day starts
and the old day ends,
There's no better time
for making amends
For all the things we sincerely regret
And wish in our hearts
we could somehow forget.

Repent

I tell you that in the same way there will be more rejoicing in heaven over one sinner who repents than over ninety-nine righteous persons who do not need to repent.
Luke 15:7 NIV

We all make mistakes –
It's human to err –
But no one need
ever give up in despair,
For God gives us all
a brand-new beginning,
A chance to start over
and repent of our sinning.

He forgives

And when you stand praying, if you hold anything against anyone, forgive him, so that your Father in heaven may forgive you your sins.
Mark 11:25 NIV

Christ came and dwelled among us
and He knows our every need,
And He loves and understands us
and forgives each sinful deed.

A new start

"The time has come," he said.
"The kingdom of God is near. Repent
and believe the good news!"
Mark 1:15 NIV

Each day at dawning
we have but to pray
That all of the mistakes
that we made yesterday
Will be blotted out
and forgiven by grace,
For God, in His mercy,
will completely efface
All that is past,
and He'll grant a new start
To all who are truly repentant at heart.

Willing to forgive

*Repent of this wickedness and
pray to the Lord. Perhaps he
will forgive you for having
such a thought in your heart.*
Acts 8:22 NIV

Well may we pause
in awesome-like wonder
That our Father in heaven,
who dwells far asunder,
Could still remain willing
to freely forgive
The shabby, small lives
we so selfishly live.

The gift

Forgive us our sins, for we also
forgive everyone who sins against
us. And lead us not into temptation.
Luke 11:4 NIV

This is the gift of God's
limitless love,
A gift that we all
are so unworthy of,
But God gave it to us
and all we need do
Is to ask God's forgiveness
and begin life anew.

Forgive one another

Bear with each other and forgive
whatever grievances you may
have against one another.
Forgive as the Lord forgave you.
Colossians 3:13 NIV

Since God forgives us,
we too must forgive
And resolve to do better
each day that we live
By constantly trying
to be like Him more nearly
To trust in His wisdom
and to love Him more dearly.

Renew me

But if you do not forgive men their sins,
your Father will not forgive your sins.
Matthew 6:15 NIV

GOOD MORNING GOD!

You are ushering in another day,
untouched and freshly new,
So here I am to ask You,
God, if You'll renew me, too.
Forgive the many errors
that I made yesterday
And let me try again,
dear God, to walk closer
in Thy way.

Through His name

All the prophets testify, about him that
everyone who believes in him receives
forgiveness of sins through his name.
Acts 10:43 NIV

In Thy goodness and mercy,
look down on this weak, erring one
And tell me that I am forgiven
for all I've so willfully done.

Grant me peace

Forgive us our debts, as we also
have forgiven our debtors.
Matthew 6:12 NIV

Oh God of love, who sees us all,
You are so great – we are so small.
Hear this universal prayer
crying to You in despair –
Save my soul, grant me peace,
let my restless murmurings cease.
God of love, forgive – forgive,
teach me how to truly live.

God's children

If you forgive anyone, I also forgive him.
And what I have forgiven – if there was
anything to forgive – I have forgiven in
the sight of Christ for your sake, in order
that Satan might not outwit us.
For we are not unaware of his schemes.
2 Corinthians 2:10, 11 NIV

We are all God's children
and He loves us, every one.
He freely and completely
forgives all that we have done,
Asking only if we're ready
to follow where He leads,
Content that in His wisdom
He will answer all our needs.

The joy you give

For you make me glad by your
deeds, O Lord; I sing for joy
at the works of your hands.
Psalm 92:4 NIV

Time is not measured
by the years that you live
But by the deeds that you
do and the joy that you give –
And each day as it comes
brings a chance to each one
To love to the fullest,
leaving nothing undone
That would brighten
the life or lighten the load
Of some weary traveler
lost on life's road.

Songs of joy

*Those living far away fear
your wonders; where morning
dawns and evening fades
you call forth songs of joy.*
Psalm 65:8 NIV

Thank You, God, for little things
that often come my way –
The unexpected little joys
that brighten up my day –
And thank You for the beauty
around me everywhere –
The gentle rain
and glistering dew,
the sunshine and the air.

Joy in your presence

You have made known to me
the paths of life; you will fill
me with joy in your presence.
Acts 2:28 NIV

To kneel in Your presence
makes me feel blessed,
For I know that You know
all my needs best,
And it fills me with joy just
to linger with You,
As my soul You replenish
and my heart You renew.

Unexpected joys

Sing to him a new song;
play skilfully, and shout for joy.
Psalm 33:3 NIV

Into our lives come many things
to break the dull routine, the things we
had not planned on that happen
unforseen the unexpected little joys
that are scattered on our way, success
we did not count on or a rare, fulfilling
day, a catchy, lilting melody that makes
us want to dance, a nameless exaltation
of enchantment and romance, an
unsought word of kindness, a
compliment or two that set
the eyes to gleaming like
crystal drops of dew.

Perfector of our faith

*Let us fix our eyes on Jesus, the
author and perfecter of our faith, who
for the joy set before him endured the
cross, scorning its shame, and sat down
at the right hand of the throne of God.*

Hebrews 12:2 NIV

God gives us not only
joy and happiness
but the faith to meet each trial
Not with fear and trepidation
but with an inner smile.

Memories

*For everything there is
a season, and a time for
every matter under heaven.*
Ecclesiastes 3:1 RSV

Memories are priceless possessions
that time can never destroy,
For it is in happy remembrance
that the heart finds its greatest joy.

Power in belief

He gives power to the faint,
and to him who has no
might he increases strength.
Isaiah 40:29 RSV

God gives us a power
we so seldom employ
For we're so unaware
it is filled with such joy.
The gift that God gives us
is anticipation,
Which we can fulfill
with sincere expectation,
For there's power in belief
when we think we will find
Joy for the heart
and peace for the mind.

Open the door

I am the door; if any one enters
by me, he will be saved, and will
go in and out and find pasture.
John 10:9 RSV

We open the door
to let joy walk through
When we learn to expect
the best and most, too,
And believing we'll find a happy surprise
Makes reality out of a fancied surmise.

Without doubt

*Jesus immediately reached out
his hand and caught him,
saying to him "O man of little
faith, why did you doubt?"*
Matthew 14:31 RSV

To know and believe
without question or doubt
That no matter what happens
God is there to help out
Is to hold in your hand the golden key
To peace and joy and serenity.

Higher heights

The steps of man are from
the Lord, and he establishes him
in whose way he delights.
Psalm 37:23 RSV

An aching heart is but a steppingstone
To greater joy than you've ever known,
For things that cause the heart to ache
Until you think that it must break
Become the strength by which we climb
To higher heights that are sublime.

Simple things

Of old thou didst lay the
foundation of the earth, and the
heavens are the work of thy hands.
Psalm 102:25

In simple things
may you always find
Joys of the very greatest kind:
The good, green earth
beneath your feet,
The air you breathe,
the food you eat,
Some work to do,
a goal to win,
A sense of peace
deep down within.

Daily miracles

*And we have the prophetic word
made more sure. You will do well to
pay attention to this as to a lamp shining
in a dark place, until the day dawns and
the morning star rises in your hearts.*
2 Peter 1:19 RSV

The sun rising in the sky as night
is tucked away, the joy of just
awakening to a new and untouched
day, the beauty of the dawning, the
freshness of the dew, the inky clouds
of darkness becoming azure blue are
daily little miracles that speak of God's
great glory – for who can watch the
dawning and doubt
the Easter story?